Tell Me A Story, Grandma

Tell Me A Story, Grandma

Childhood Stories Of Joyce

Avril Sabine

Cracked Acorn Productions
Australia

Tell Me A Story, Grandma

Childhood Stories Of Joyce

Published by

Cracked Acorn Productions

PO Box 1365

Gympie, Queensland 4570

Australia

978-1-925617-60-3 (Kindle)

978-1-925617-61-0 (EPUB)

978-1-925131-59-8 (Large Print)

Genre: Memoir

Copyright 2016 © Avril Sabine

Cover design by Caitlyn Petersen

All rights reserved

For Grandma, who was always willing to tell me about when she was a child.

Joyce

Born April 1926

Joyce's childhood was during an era when sugar cane was cut by hand, not everyone had electricity or running water, recycling was more a necessity than a lifestyle and people dressed up when calling on their neighbours. This is a collection of stories told to her granddaughter when she was a child, fascinated by a world so different from her own.

This story was written by an Australian author using Australian spelling.

Foreword

One of my favourite parts about staying at my grandma's, when I was young, was listening to stories of when she was a child. I was fascinated. The world she described was such a different place. Alien and unknown to me. There were of course similarities, but there were so many things I struggled to imagine. I asked a million questions, trying to picture the places and events Grandma described.

During primary school I started

collecting Grandma's stories, writing them down and asking her to tell them to me over and over again so I could check what I'd written. It wasn't until I had my own children that I asked if she could tell me the stories once more, so I could check I'd written them accurately, before I shared them with my children. They enjoyed them as much as I did. A glimpse into a world so different from our own.

Although Grandma has passed away, she lives on in my memories and in the stories she shared with me when I was a child.

Avril Sabine.
2016.

1

I was born in Rockhampton in April 1926. We lived there until I was about two when we moved to Gladstone. I have no idea why we moved. I was too little at the time to know and children weren't told things like that. The house we moved to was an ordinary weatherboard house that was sealed and lined inside. There were six steps with railings that led to a verandah that ran across the front of the house and palings went all around the bottom of the house so you couldn't crawl underneath it. At the front Mum had two large ferns, one on either side of the door. Dad had made her stands of polished wood for her to put them on and the ferns were really large and beautiful. The back door of the house led into the laundry. I remember drawing in the dirt of the floor when Mum put me down there on the potty while I was being toilet trained.

We lived about three blocks from the main street, but close enough to the creek that my brothers went down to the mud flats to play. They liked to chase little mud crabs and watch them run back to their homes. Sometimes they brought them home to show us.

2

While we lived in Gladstone, we sometimes went to the movies of an evening. We didn't go often, only every few months. At the most it was two or three times a year. I remember the whole family walked to the movies. Mum, Dad, my two brothers, my sister and me. My parents had lost two boys before I was born so there was only the four of us and I was the youngest. They lost their first son when he was eight-months-old and the second one when he was six-years-old. My sister was their third child and now the oldest and then came my two brothers.

Gladstone had a hill and we walked up the main street, past houses and shops, along a bitumen road with dirt edges. The theatre was a little bit down the other side of the hill. It had canvas seats fitted on a wooden frame, sort of like deck chairs. They were fixed to the concrete floors so they couldn't be moved. Some of the seats were singles and some were doubles.

Each time before the movie started, they played 'God Save the King' and we all had to stand up. Once the song was over, there was a newsreel and what we called a comic. Eventually they became known as cartoons. The movie was then played. I don't remember any of the movies from when I was little, only when I was older and went to see movies like 'Blossoms in the Dust'. They were all black and white movies and I usually fell asleep before the movie ended and Dad had to carry me home. It was a fair walk, but luckily it was mostly down hill all the way.

3

When I was about four I had diphtheria. All the family had to have their throats swabbed to see if they had it and we found out my brother, Len, was the carrier. We were told carriers didn't get sick. I was put in hospital in isolation and hated it because my family weren't allowed to visit. I don't know if Len was isolated too, but he wasn't in the hospital I was in. The hospital had a verandah and that was as close as my family could come to me. An entire verandah width apart. When he visited, Dad put a slab of chocolate in under the railing of the verandah and slid it across the floor to where I was. He didn't visit every day, but when he did visit he usually brought a slab of chocolate with him. One day, while I was in the hospital, Dad visited when I had a towel around my head. He was worried they'd cut my hair so Dad went to ask matron why my hair was wrapped in a towel. He found out it was because I had head lice and they'd wrapped my hair up because they'd put kerosene on it to kill them. The nurses were the only ones allowed in to me and they all had to wear masks on their faces. I don't remember exactly how long I was in the hospital, but it seemed like I was left alone for a very long time.

4

During our childhood whenever anyone got the measles, everyone sent their kids over to play with them so they could get the measles out of the way. Lots of kids ended up catching measles that way, but I can't remember my brothers, sister or me catching them. I also don't remember anyone I knew being immunised.

5

Mum regularly gave us a teaspoon of yellow mixture to keep our blood pure and prevent school sores. It was sulphur put into syrup to help disguise its taste. I can't remember how often she gave it to us, but I think it was only once a month. We all had to line up for our dose. Every Saturday morning we also had to line up for a dose of castor oil. It had a terrible taste. We took it with a pinch of salt. First we put the salt on our tongue and then took the oil. It was meant to keep our bowels regular and it tasted terrible. My brothers teased me that I took more than a pinch of salt. That I had more salt than oil.

I never saw our parents having either the castor oil or the sulphur. Only us kids had to have them.

6

Even though Dad had a truck, we walked most places. The truck, which was a Chevy, was for Dad's work. He was a carpenter. He built houses and even went out west to build wool sheds and cotton ginneries. Sometimes he was away for ages working. He also built what we called baby-minders. They were a little bit like baby walkers, but without the seat or toys. The baby-minders were made of plain pine and castors. They had a square frame with a few pieces so the baby couldn't fall out or through them. Babies stood in the minders and pushed them along when they first started walking. They were to help them learn to walk rather than for them to sit and play in.

7

I don't remember how old I was, but when I was little I was scared of the steam train. We called it a Puffing Billy. It was a great big black train with gold coloured bands around it in places. The station was covered with a big roof and when the train came in, it made a loud noise and smoke filled the area near the roof. When it came into the station I hid behind my mum. We didn't go there very much. When we did go, we always wore our best clothes. Sometimes there were a lot of people and at other times there was only a handful.

The railway station platform was made of concrete and there were seats, pots with ferns and hanging baskets of flowers. It was quite a large station. The train didn't have a dining carriage so they stopped for about twenty minutes so people could use the tearoom for refreshments. The tearoom had tables covered in white tablecloths.

The station also had a Stationmaster's office, a goods office where goods that came off the train were stored, toilets and a room for people to sit in while they were waiting to catch the train. When it was time for the train to depart, they rang a bell to let everyone know. It was a large hand bell and the stationmaster stood where the passengers got in the carriage. He rang the bell a couple of times to let everyone know it was time to leave. They knew how many had to get on. The stationmaster also blew his whistle and called out, "All aboard." When everyone was on, he waved a green flag to signal the driver to leave.

8

During the week, while my brothers and sister were at school, I stayed home and played with my teddy. He was twelve inches high and golden coloured. I called him Teddy. I liked to take him for drives in my red pedal car and I drove it up and down the verandah. I also had tea parties with him.

Porcelain tea sets were very expensive so I had a little set made of tin. It was unpainted inside, but the outside was painted yellow. Red flowers with green leaves were painted nearly all the way around the outside. There were cups and saucers, teaspoons and even a teapot. Sometimes I put real water in the teapot, but never tea. I didn't have a little table of my own, but sometimes I sat at a small box and other times I sat on the steps facing the house, with my legs dangling through and the tea set on the next step up. Sometimes my best friends came to play. When I was five, I went to their house to play every Saturday morning.

I loved Saturdays. I put on one of my dresses and hurried out to have my breakfast. My hair didn't take long to do because it was short and curly. I didn't grow it until I was older. The dresses I wore were an inch or two past my knees and buttoned down the back to my waist.

Mum had to help me button my dresses. Each dress was white with tiny flowers printed all over it and had a sash at the waist. One dress had a rose bud print. I don't think I ever got in trouble for getting them dirty when I played outside and I know we sometimes got dirty playing hidey.

I didn't always wear dresses. Sometimes I wore Clara Bow skirts with a blouse. They were a skirt on a waistband and had straps that were an inch and a half wide attached to the back. These were then crossed over at the back, came over the shoulders and buttoned onto the band at the front. Clara Bow was a famous film actress.

After I had breakfast of rolled oats made into porridge with sugar and milk on it, I visited my friends. They were only three houses away so I was allowed to walk there by myself. The youngest was five like me and her sister was seven. They had an older sister and brother. Sometimes my sister went with me to play with their older sister. My sister was eight years older than me and neither her or their sister liked to play games with little kids so I didn't have much to do with their older sister.

My friends had a lovely back yard. There was a little gully running through it and a hill we could roll down. We spent a lot of time rolling down that hill. There were also lots of good places to hide when we played hidey. The best hiding places were in the bushes and under the house.

Sometimes, I was invited to have dinner at their house. You had to use your best manners when you ate there. Their father had a cane stick, like the ones that the kewpie dolls at the show came on. If you slouched or put your elbows on the table he reached over and tapped you on the shoulder. He was a nice man and never hit us with it, just reminded us to use our manners. We also had to say 'may I please leave the table' when we were finished. Some of the other games I played with my friends was skipping, dolls, hopscotch and pretend tea parties.

9

When I was old enough, I had to go to school. We still lived in Gladstone and I was there for a couple of years of school. I didn't like it one bit. The first day I cried so hard they got my sister out of her class and she was mad at me. It was a big school with both primary and high school students. We had slates at school and wrote on them with chalk.

10

Around the age of five, the circus came to town. When the circus came they had a parade through the street. The animals were in their cages and they slowly travelled down the main street so everyone could see what sort of animals were in the circus. The elephants, horses and camels walked in the parade too. The elephants led the parade and the clowns, acrobats and other circus people were all dressed in their costumes.

The main street of Gladstone has a

bit of a hill and I was standing near the top. I could see everything from there and at the start of the parade all the animals and people looked so small. As they slowly marched along they began to get bigger and bigger until they were close enough the elephants towered over me. I was so frightened I ran and hid in the cafe, behind the counter, and missed the rest of the parade. Afterwards my brothers teased me about hiding from the elephants. I don't remember if we went to that particular circus, but we did go to a couple of circuses while we lived in Gladstone.

The circus always set up on the mud flats. They had a big tent and inside was a sawdust ring in the centre with stools set up around the outside of the ring. The stools were planks of wood on metal stands and if you leaned back, you were leaning on the legs of the person behind you.

What most stuck in my mind about going to the circus when I was little was seeing the lions and tigers let into the cage in the ring. I was always scared they were going to get out. I kept thinking that if they did, they were going to get me. It never occurred to me that they might attack the other people at the circus. It was always a relief when they went back in their own cages.

11

Every Sunday morning while we lived in Gladstone, Mum gave my brother and me two shillings. While Mum cooked dinner, which is what we called the midday meal, we walked to the shop. Everyone called it the Chinaman's shop. His brother grew vegetables out the back of the shop. It was a single storey shop that you walked straight into off the footpath, unlike some of the other shops that you had to step up into. It was in the main street of Gladstone amongst other businesses. I don't know what other shops were around it, I only had eyes for the lollies. We always walked on a little track going from the back street between other buildings, along the side of the shop, onto the footpath and in the front door.

At the front of the shop were glass windows and you could see all the different things inside that were for sale. He sold things like groceries, bread and the newspaper. I don't remember everything he had to sell, I was only interested in the lollies we went to buy. Each time we bought a big brown paper packet of lollies and took them home to have that afternoon. We all sat on Mum's bed and shared them out. This was while Dad was working up north.

The lollies were our treat for the

week and we never missed out on them. Mum never took them from us as a punishment if we didn't behave. Some of the lollies were the same as we have today, but there were also different ones. The ones like we have today tasted a lot better back then and seemed to have more flavour. Some of the lollies we could get ten for a penny, like peppermint sticks and musk sticks. There was also a lolly called a lucky slipper, which was two or three for a penny. It was made out of a soft lolly, a bit like a marshmallow, but different. Where the foot went into the slipper there was a piece of paper stuck over it. When you pulled off the paper you found a present like a locket or ring. Another lolly I liked was a Kurl. It was a white peppermint toffee covered in chocolate. It was about four or five inches long and about one and a half inches wide and wrapped in silver paper. It only cost a penny. There were twelve pennies to a shilling so we could get a lot of lollies for two shillings.

12

We couldn't get lollies or food at school like today as there wasn't a tuckshop. This meant we always had to take our own lunch. There might have been a little shop across the road from the school that sold lollies and stuff, but it didn't make lunches for the kids to have at lunchtime. We didn't take anything special to eat at school. For little lunch, in the morning, we usually had a couple of biscuits or a piece of cake. For big lunch it was sandwiches with

Vegemite or peanut paste. We didn't take drink bottles to school. We had our own cup we filled at the tap when we wanted a drink. On sports day they tied a string through the handle of our cups and the girls hung theirs around their necks so they hung down to the waist and the boys tied theirs around their waist and untied them when they wanted a drink.

13

On Saturdays while we were living in Gladstone we sat on the steps and waited for the ice cream man, a penny clutched in our hands. We listened to the tinkle of his little silver bell and waited as it grew louder. A chestnut pony pulled his ice cream cart, which had sides that went to about waist high with an awning over it to keep the sun out. There was a counter top and the ice cream man served us from there. It was a penny an ice cream. They were a single vanilla scoop in a 'v' shaped cone. There were no toppings or other flavours or special cones. We all had the same. The ice creams were always cold and firm so he probably had to use an icebox to keep the ice cream cold. I don't know for sure because I never saw behind the counter.

The only iceboxes I ever saw were ones in houses, so I don't know what it would have looked like if he had one. Iceboxes in houses were like a cupboard with a full block of ice put in the top. The cupboards were made of brown polished timber and were about three foot high. The water from the melting ice ran through to a tray underneath. Only people who could afford the ice to keep them cold had them. They used them for things like butter and milk. We didn't own one.

14

We had a pet koala for seven years. He was a baby when Dad caught him in the Proserpine bush when I was about six. He brought him with him when he came home before Christmas. Dad worked up at Noorlah and Caping sidings, unloading cane off the trains onto the trucks to go to the mill. Noorlah was on the south side of the O'Connell River and Caping was on the north side of the river. The closest town was Proserpine.

Dad went up north to make money quickly so he could get out of debt. His business partner had cleaned out their joint business bank account and left him with all the bills. They'd been building houses and sheds together.

Dad carted cane around Noorlah and Caping area for about two or three years. Since the cane harvesting season went from June to almost Christmas he didn't get home very often. It was one of those times that Dad brought the koala back to Gladstone for us and built him a cage. We called him Teddy. When we took the train north to see Dad, on the school holidays, Teddy went with us. He was charged his weight and a half on the train and his cage went in what was called the dog box.

Farmers had barracks on their farms that workers stayed in during the crushing. Sometimes the barracks were the original farmhouse the farmer had lived in until he'd built a good house. Other times the barracks were a shed with corrugated walls, push out corrugated windows and a concrete floor. When my father carted cane for the farmers he stayed in their barracks.

When it wasn't cane season, Dad went to Bloomsbury to work with the timber. I don't know if he worked for the railway or the sawmill, but all the iron bark trees they cut down were sent to the sawmill to be cut into railway sleepers. When they cut down the trees they had to take the bark off, cut them into the correct size and load them onto trucks. The timber was then taken to the railway siding where it was loaded onto the train trucks waiting to take it to the sawmill. The siding was on a loop line, which meant it was a line coming off the main one and then looping back onto it. If there were no train trucks there, they stockpiled the timber to be put onto the open train trucks later. From there, the timber was taken to the sawmill in Mackay. I believe the timber was then sent from the mill to wherever they needed sleepers for the railway line.

15

We only visited Dad during school holidays, when he was cutting timber, never when he was carting cane. Bloomsbury didn't have many houses. There was a railway station, a stationmaster's house, butchers, grocery shop, a post office with a home upstairs, a schoolhouse for the teacher to live in, a highset primary school and a few other houses. It was a very small settlement. They eventually built houses for the railway workers, but while we were there, the railway workers lived in tents with their families. Today all the railway workers' houses are gone.

When we visited Dad in Bloomsbury we stayed in a big tent and a grass hut. I was always scared fires would come through and the grass hut would burn down while we were in it. The tent had a canvas top and sides, the ends open. There were no zips, flyscreen or floor in it. We had to put down a tarp to cover the grass. We used the big tent to eat under, but slept in the grass hut. The hut had a dirt floor and it was made of thatched grass.

Our beds were called bunks, but were more like a hammock. Four sapling posts, with forks in the top of them, were put in the ground, two at each end with space between them. A sack bag was threaded onto two straight posts and each end of the posts were sat in the forks of the saplings. The sack bags hung on the two pieces of timber in a way that made a little hollow in them so you didn't fall out. Sack bags were woven out of a type of twine and were thicker than hessian, which was a light see-through type of sack. We didn't see many hessian bags when I was a kid. Even sugar from the mill came in sack bags. Small bags for flour were made of calico fabric, but the large bags of flour came in sack bags too.

My parents, my sister and I all slept in sack bag bunks. My brothers slept on a mattress on the back of Dad's truck. Sometimes little bats came into the hut of a night and my brothers had to chase them out.

16

When I was about seven or eight, Dad decided to lease a farm at Caping and we all left Gladstone and moved up north to live on the farm. We took Teddy with us in his cage, but had to leave some of our furniture behind because it wouldn't fit in the farmhouse. We left it with Dad's younger brother, who lived in Gladstone. The rest of their family were scattered around the countryside, having moved from

Mackay where they'd been born and raised.

On the farm, Dad mainly grew vegetables like cabbages, tomatoes and potatoes. While he worked the vegetable farm Dad continued to cart cane for the farmers as he didn't make enough money from the farm to support us.

The house we lived in had a dirt floor and corrugated iron walls and roof. There was a long kitchen and three bedrooms. My parents had one room, my sister and I the other and my brothers shared the third room. The bedrooms had sack bag bunks, except our parents' room. They had the double bed they'd brought with them from Gladstone.

The toilet was an outhouse at the back of the house, which meant it was a hole in the ground with a shelter over it. There was a wooden box placed over the drop hole with a hole cut in it for somewhere to sit when we went to the toilet. It had a lid on it to keep the flies out.

The bathroom was also outside and was a bucket shower with holes in the bottom. You had to fill it with water, hoist it up, turn the tap on and quickly have a shower before the water ran out.

The rooms weren't very big, just large enough to live in. The windows were corrugated iron and pushed out to be held open with a stick. We called them push out shutters. To keep the mosquitoes away, we put dry cow dung in a tin and lit it. The tin was moved around inside the house, depending on where the wind came from, so the smoke blew through the house. We extinguished the cow dung at bedtime and the mosquitoes came in, unless we lit a smoky fire outside to keep them away. It wasn't very pleasant, the smoke or the smell of the cow dung. We had mosquito nets to hang over our beds until most of them wore out. I don't remember us kids having them for very long.

During the time we lived there, we walked across the river to play with what we thought of as 'the rich kids'. In some ways their lives weren't much different from ours. They didn't get to town much either, they had to help out with chores and they did correspondence. Some of the chores the girls did were things like washing up, making the beds, sweeping out and helping with washing the clothes. The boys helped out in the paddock chipping, or doing chores around the farm. Chipping was using a hoe to weed the cane paddocks. Usually girls had to help around the house while boys helped outside. The things that made the neighbours wealthier than us was that they had better houses to live in, better clothes and toys and some of the families even had a governess.

By the time we moved to the vegetable farm, Teddy was living in the house. Dad put a tree stump, which had been the fork of a tree, in the kitchen for him. He didn't always stay on it and had the run of the house. He also thought the house yard was his. One day a man from the next farm came over and brought his young dog with him. Teddy came down out of his tree and chased the dog. Even though Teddy was smaller, the dog ran across the paddock towards home. Teddy didn't chase the dog all the way. Once the dog was on the run, Teddy came sauntering back and climbed up into his tree. It was the talk of the town for a while.

Dad had a beautiful camera that was only brought out for special occasions. Teddy chasing the dog and then sauntering back home would have made a good photo, but sadly it hadn't been a special occasion so the camera wasn't out.

17

While we were living on the fruit and vegetable farm I went to a fancy dress party as Silver Star Starch. Silver Star Starch was a brand of starch that was used on clothes. The bodice of my dress was made of calico and the skirt was made of crepe paper, like a tutu. The skirt had some silver paper on it, I had a wand with a silver star, a silver crown with a star and the words Silver Star Starch were written on the crown. I even had silver stars on the tops of my white socks. The school holding the fancy dress party was down the track at Bloomsbury. You didn't need to go to the Bloomsbury school to attend, anyone could go. I was the only child in my family who went. The other kids were too old to want to go to a fancy dress party. Both my parents took me and we went in Dad's Chevy truck he'd brought with him from Gladstone.

18

When I was around the age of eight or nine we moved from the fruit and vegetable farm and onto a sugar cane farm for more than ten years. The cane farm was further along and over the river from where we'd been living on the fruit and vegetable farm. Dad didn't own the farm, but worked it for someone else.

Our house was mostly made of corrugated iron. The roof, most of the walls and all of the windows except for the ones in my parents' room were corrugated iron. My parents had real glass windows. The rest of the windows were corrugated push out shutters that we propped open with a stick. The floor was concrete covered with linoleum and there were no mats or rugs. But at least we no longer had a dirt floor. The house had six rooms. There was a bedroom for my parents, one for my sister and me, a bedroom for my brothers, a dining room, a long kitchen and a storage room. The house wasn't lined and we often saw snakes in the rafters. Mainly carpet snakes, but occasionally brown snakes. My brothers shot the snakes curled up in the ceiling rafters and afterwards had to go up on the roof to fix the holes in the corrugated iron. It was safer than being bitten by a brown snake when there was no medical help nearby.

The house was partly furnished when we moved in and Mum had the furniture, which was stored at my uncle's house, brought up. It arrived in a covered train wagon at the railway siding and Dad picked it up in his truck. There was Mum's silky oak dining table, chairs and sideboard that had a mirror and they all went in the dining room with the radio. We didn't have a lounge suite so when we listened to the radio us kids sat on the floor and Mum sat on a dining chair. Dad was usually in the office he'd created at one end of their bedroom.

Their bedroom was at the end of the house and was a long room. He made shelves out of the pine boxes the kerosene came in to partition his office off from the bedroom. The shelves were filled with his papers, books and bottles with snakes and spiders preserved in liquid. We weren't allowed in that part of the house. It was Dad's place. The boxes went from the floor to nearly the roof.

Even though we listened to the radio in the dining room, we rarely ate in there. Apart from Mum sitting in one to listen to the radio, the chairs weren't used often, not even on the rare occasions we had visitors. We sat in the kitchen on the kitchen chairs for meals and also when there were visitors. The dining room was for special occasions and we didn't have many of those. Christmas was about the only time I recall using the dining room.

In the kitchen was a wooden table,

chairs and a food safe. The food safe was a wooden cupboard to keep groceries in. It had wire gauze on the sides. We also had a hanging safe. It had a little hook that it hung from and a funnel at the top to fill with water so the ants couldn't come down the hook and into the safe. Ours hung at the end of the kitchen near a window so it could get a bit of a breeze. The meat was kept cool by the breeze blowing through it. Looking back I'm surprised we didn't get sick from bacteria growing in the meat. Particularly during the heat of summer.

We had a big cast iron kettle in the kitchen that was always kept on the stove. We had to make sure it was full of water so it didn't boil dry. It had a spout and a marble in it to roll around in the bottom to keep it clean. The handle was cast iron so a rag was needed to pick it up once it had been boiled. We bought Bushels Tea, which came in a big square tin. The tin was made of metal that was painted orange with Bushels Tea written in navy blue. There were no images, just the words. Mum kept the tins and reused them. I can't remember ever having coffee in the house when I was young. Everyone drank tea.

In my room, there was a double iron bed I shared with my sister, a wardrobe and a duchess. Both the duchess and the wardrobe had mirrors. On our bed, just like all the other beds, was a fibre mattress and kapok pillows. The fibre material of the mattress was called mattress ticking. The material covering the ticking was striped black and white.

Kapok looks like raw cotton, only it's a creamy colour. It comes from around the seeds of a kapok tree. The fibre in the mattress looked like brown coconut husk, but I don't know where it came from.

Every few years housewives would 'tease' the mattress. This was a really big job. The mattress was pulled apart and the fibre was boiled in the boiler used to do the laundry. It was then laid out to dry. Once it was dried and repacked in the mattress, the mattress was sewn up and all the little buttons that kept the fibre from moving about were sewn back on. Some people had kapok mattresses, which were firm but soft. The fibre mattresses were very firm, but comfortable enough. Cot mattresses were made the same way.

The laundry was at the back of the

house, set about six metres away from it. At one end was a set of cement tubs and at the other end was a bathroom. There was no running water so we never did the washing in the laundry. That was done at the river once a week. Further away from the house than the laundry was the toilet. It had a corrugated iron roof and walls with a wooden door and a cement floor. The actual toilet was like a square box with a lid and a door on the front to take the pan in and out. Under the lid was a proper pine seat. The toilet pan was for the girls and the boys went bush.

19

We did our washing every Monday, unless Mum was busy in the paddock. We loaded the washing into two galvanised tubs. They were both about eighteen inches high with handles. The smaller one was around twenty-four inches in diameter and the bigger one was about thirty inches. They were also used to bring the washing back from the river. If we had too much washing to fit it all in the tubs, we filled pillowcases with washing too. Along with the washing, we took an empty tank to bring water back to the house for washing the dishes, our hands and ourselves. The little tank was made of corrugated iron and it took about twenty gallons to fill it. We used galvanised iron buckets, which were about a gallon in size, to fill the tank by hand. Everything was put onto a slide to take it down to the river. The slide was built from timber and looked a bit like a thin platform. It had no wheels, only a flat piece of iron underneath so it could slide along the grass when pulled by the horse.

Sometimes my brothers came down to the river and backed the horse around so the slide was right at the water's edge to make it easier to fill the tank with fresh water. We all took turns at filling it. Mostly Mum and I filled it and my brothers only helped if they were working nearby. We had a rainwater tank at the house, but it was only for cooking and drinking water. For everything else we had the water from the river. The rainwater tank was the only drinking water we had so we had to be careful with it in case there wasn't enough rain. If we ran out of water in the little tank during the week, that meant no water for baths. We always had to be careful of how much water we used.

To get to the river from the house we had to walk down a hill, across a cane paddock, through a gully and across another cane paddock before we reached the freshwater river. Everything was washed. Towels, sheets and clothes. Our copper boiler was left in a paddock near the river and it sat on old leaf springs from a truck that were laid across rocks.

We didn't have washing powder. We had bars of soap. To soapy up the boiler we cut up about half a cake of washing soap and threw it in the boiler where it melted. All our whites were put in the boiler while our coloured clothes were washed by hand with a scrubbing board. The whites were done on the scrubbing board before they were boiled. All the cane working clothes were boiled as well. The Bonds singlets, 'Can't Tear 'Em' shirts, long pants, khaki shorts and Mum's overalls. By the time we finished washing our hands were red. I first started helping with the washing when we moved to the sugar cane farm.

When we lived in town, Mum had a boiler on a stand in the back yard. It was the same as washing at the farm. The only difference was that in town she didn't have to go so far or bring water back for the house.

Once we'd washed everything we put it back in the tubs to take it to the house and hang it up. Our clothesline was a wire strung between two mango trees with a prop in the middle so the washing didn't drag on the ground.

20

We recycled a lot of things. Dad made a washing up basin out of a kerosene tin cut in two. Mum made tea towels from flour bags with her treadle sewing machine. She also made waggas. She pulled the sack bags, the potatoes came in, apart and joined two together, using coloured material for a trim to bind the edges. We had them on our beds for a bedspread. Two sacks were big enough for a single bed. My sister and I had a floral trim, but I don't remember what my brothers had. Mum trimmed them with whatever material she could find or had left over from other things. The sack bags were boiled in the boiler until they became soft and beige-like in colour. Sort of like a dark calico colour. As well as the waggas, we had a sheet on the mattress and a grey, scratchy blanket on top of us. We also used the sack bags for mats at the doors, in the kitchen in front of where we washed up and on the floor beside our beds.

21

Because we were so far out of town, my brother and I did correspondence. It was mailed to us and we got black and red ink powder that we made up with water, a pack of nibs and a wooden pen to fit the nibs onto. When we finished one lot of work, we sent it in to be corrected while we did the next lot we'd been sent. I did correspondence till about the end of primary school when I was twelve or thirteen. After that, I helped out more around the house and farm. Mum helped us with our correspondence during the week if she wasn't needed in the paddock. I don't know exactly how big the farm was, but it was divided up into four large paddocks.

My parents both worked in the paddocks. The sugar cane farm was very hard work. Some days they were out there from sun up to sun down, only coming in for the midday meal. There was always a lot to do. Ploughing the paddock, planting the cane, weeding it and then they started cutting it by hand in June. Sometimes we didn't finish cutting until Christmas day. Each year we sent in several tonnes of green cane for a bonus, but it was harder to cut because we had to cut the thrash off with a cane knife. When we burned the rest of the cane before cutting it, the thrash burned off, making it easier. The tops had to be removed from the cane so we kept them for our horses to eat.

It was hard to cut the cane. First we cut the cane off at the ground with a cane knife, one at a time. Then we twisted it to cut the top off. After that we threw the stick into the bundle of cut cane. The tops were taken up to the shed and put through the chaff cutter for the horses. It was like a big wheel with a tray to put the chaff on. You pushed the tray with one hand towards the cutters, which were on the big wheel. This wheel was turned with the other hand. Molasses was dribbled over the tops before it was fed to the horses. We all took turns using the chaff cutter, even me. It was a big wheel and a tiring job to do.

When the cane was cut, it was gathered into bundles. Several rows of growing cane went into a bundle and the lorry, which is what we called the truck, was parked between them. Before any of the cane was loaded onto the lorry two slings were put on it first, approximately three feet apart. The slings were a wire rope about an inch thick with a loop at each end. These loops were so the hook on the crane at the siding could be attached to it. The bundles of cane were then picked up and carted on the shoulder to the lorry. Sometimes when the bundles were lifted snakes fell out or large spiders crawled across your hat.

When the stack got higher on the lorry, a little ladder was leaned up against the back of the truck to climb up and put the rest of the bundles on. Once the lorry was loaded, the rope on the sling was tightened so the cane couldn't fall out.

Cane grew back again after it was cut and the farmers did that a few times before they had to plough it out and let the paddock lay idle for a season before it could be planted again. First year cane was called plant cane and the following seasons of cane were called return cane. Both Mum and Dad wore overalls when they were working with the cane.

22

While we lived on the sugar cane farm, our lorry was a red Chevrolet with an open cabin and a windscreen. When we first moved there we didn't have a tractor. We ploughed the paddocks with harrows drawn by horses. This was to get rid of the last of the stubble from the previous lot of cane. First we only had a single plough disk, but we eventually upgraded to a double. It had a place to sit on while you guided the horse and the double mould board threw dirt out on both sides of the furrow and made a ridge. The single mould board we started with threw dirt to one side of the furrow and the farmer had to walk behind. Over the years we ended up with a lot of different implements for the horse to pull, including a scuffler and a whisk. They were all made of metal.

When we first started planting cane, we had to do it by hand. The long sticks of sugar cane were cut into foot long lengths and were carried by the armful. They were dropped in a good stride apart in the drill, the shallow trench made to plant the cane. Later on we got a stick planter. It was drawn by the horse and one person sat on the front, guiding the horse and positioning the planter, while another sat on the planter and put in the large sticks of cane. It cut and planted the cane. The paddocks were uneven, the country hilly, and the lever had to be raised or lowered to keep the planter level. One day when I was guiding the horses, instead of putting it in the position to lift the planter, I lowered it and Dad tumbled off the back. He didn't yell at me, but he did make me plant the rest of that row by hand.

Later on we got a tractor. It was dark green and could have been a Fordson or Ellis Chambers. It had metal tyres with prongs for grip.

23

When the lorry was loaded with the bundles of cane, Dad drove it to the railway siding. The cane then went in train trucks that were like big open wagons. There were two different sizes. FG, which fitted two lorry loads and a H, which fitted three lorry loads. The cane was taken off the lorry by hooking the wire rope up to a horse. By using a train derrick, that was driven by a horse going round and round, they were able to move the cane from the lorry to the train wagon. The derrick was a crane fixed in place that the train stopped under. At the end of the season the horse had worn a ditch from all the work it had done.

When the cane was loaded into the train wagon the sling was given back to the farmer so he could load up another lot of cane. There was a fellow at the rail siding and he built a wall with the cane to stop it from falling down while he waited for the next lot of cane to be brought in and loaded. The man at the siding also filled in a card that he slid into a metal holder at the end of the train wagon. It said which farmer owned the cane, what variety of cane and if it was plant cane or return cane. The sugar mill used the card so they knew how much to pay the farmers. Some of the varieties of cane I remember were Badilla, EK and Pinda.

When the cane arrived at the mill, they weighed the cane and tested its CCS to help them work out what to pay the farmers. The CCS measured how good the cane juice was. Plant cane always had a higher CCS than return cane. Dad had a gadget on the farm that he wound some cut cane through and the juice fell into the container. It had a little thermometer like thing that told us what the CCS was.

Plant cane was the first lot of cane cut from cane planted in a paddock. Return cane was cane that had grown back after the cane had been cut the first time. A bit like when grass is mowed and then grows back. This could be done many times but the return cane wasn't as good as the plant cane so the farmer didn't make as much money from it. Farmers only grew return cane one or two years, depending on if it was a good crop the first time.

If the crushing was finished, which is what we called the cane harvesting season, and you hadn't brought your entire crop in, what was left in the paddock was called stand over cane. The next year that was the first lot cut. The farmer checked the CCS before they sent it in. If it was low they wouldn't get as much money for it when it was sent in to be crushed. Crushing was how the juice was extracted from the cane at the sugar mill.

24

When we weren't doing chores, or helping on the farm, me and my brother, who was two years older than me, played. We played under a mango tree making roads, fences and paddocks where we drove our little tin cars. They were painted different colours and their wheels moved. Most of them were painted red or blue. We also had to play outside when our parents had visitors. If they had kids they played outside with us too. A popular saying was 'children are seen, but not heard'. It was more of a rule than only something people said.

Children had to address adults as Mr or Mrs and their surname. You never called them by their first name. We didn't even know the first name of most adults.

25

As well as the sugar cane, we also grew corn to feed the chooks and in winter we grew a paddock of potatoes. We graded the potatoes and kept the smaller ones for our family and put the rest into sacks, sewn up with twine, to sell. The whole family helped.

I had chores that I had to do every day. I washed the dishes and made smoko, which is what we now call morning tea, and took it down to the paddock to my parents. Sometimes I made patty cakes in the wood stove, or if Mum had made cakes or biscuits on the weekend I took some of them, or I made sandwiches with the fresh bread Mum had baked.

Sometimes my older brothers worked on the farm, but mostly they had their own jobs working for other farmers. My sister worked for the farmer's wife across the river. She did housework, washing, ironing and helped out with their two little boys. We didn't have anyone else working on the farm, which is why Mum had to help. I also had to feed and water the chooks and pigs, collect the eggs and bring in the calves each night.

Once a week I rode my bike to the railway siding to collect the mail. It was three or four miles away. We not only got our mail on the train, but also our meat and groceries. Meat came out every Friday night wrapped in white butcher's paper and placed in a sugar bag. Our groceries came out once a month in a big pine crate from Mackay. We didn't have a phone so Mum wrote a grocery list and posted it in our private mailbag. We also didn't have electricity during any of the years we lived on the farm. None of our neighbours had electricity either as the powerlines didn't go out our way. Some of the more well off neighbours had generators to power things.

For cooking we had a wood stove and our lights were kerosene or carbide. The kerosene lights were known as a hurricane lantern and the carbide lamps had a lower chamber filled with calcium carbide and an upper chamber filled with water. Mum was the one who filled up the lights. We didn't have a kerosene fridge until my brothers had been working for other farmers for awhile. They bought it for Mum one Christmas as there were never any birthday presents, only Christmas presents. With a fridge we were able to have ice blocks made from milk or fruit. We felt rich, like we had it made. We had lots of fruit trees on the farm so there was always plenty of fruit to make ice blocks. We also grew our own vegetables.

We had a wireless, which is what we called the radio. It was big, about three feet high, two feet wide and made of polished wood. Mum kept it polished with the same polish she used on the rest of the furniture, like the sideboard, dining table and duchesses.

We had to have a broadcast

listener's licence, which had to be renewed every year. Everyone who owned a wireless had to pay for a listener's licence. The wireless was run off a car battery and we used the truck battery to run the wireless. If Dad was using the truck, we couldn't listen to the wireless. Other farmers, who were better off than us, had a battery for their truck and one for their wireless. If the battery went flat of a night time while we were listening to the wireless we had to wait until it was used in the truck the next day for it to be recharged. Dad was the only one allowed to bring the battery in out of his truck. One time when he pulled the wireless away from the wall to put the battery in, there was a snake curled up in the back. Every night we listened to the serial 'Dad and Dave' on the wireless and during the week, when my parents came in for the midday meal, we sometimes listened to the serial 'Blue Hills'.

I remember one day when I tried to turn the wireless dial so we could listen to 'Blue Hills' and it wouldn't turn. Dad pulled the wireless out from the corner and took a snake out of the open back. It was wrapped around the part that moved the dial, which is why it wouldn't turn.

If the battery was getting flat, you had to get close to hear the wireless. Sometimes Mum listened to another serial when she wasn't working in the paddock cutting cane and occasionally she listened to the news. We didn't use it to listen to music as Mum had a gramophone. It had to be wound up every time you put a record on. There was one song on each side of the record.

Since my sister didn't ride a horse and couldn't ride a bike, she stayed with the family she worked for during the week. Dad dropped her off and collected her while he was carting cane. She left Monday morning and came back Friday night. I tried to teach her how to ride a bike, but she couldn't get it right. I never worked away from the house like my sister did. When my sister came home from work on the weekends she taught me how to dance while we listened to records on Mum's gramophone.

She taught me how to waltz to 'The Blue Danube Waltz'. There were other steps she showed me as well. I was only ten or eleven when she taught me to dance since she left the cane farm when she married at twenty, when I was twelve. I don't think my Dad was happy my sister married. Only Mum went to the wedding. She brought him home a piece of wedding cake and a glass of wine and placed them on the table in his office. He left them there until the wine dried up in the glass and something ate the cake.

26

Dad drove the truck every day, as there was always something he needed to do in it. He used it for carting cane, carting the cut cane plants to the paddock to plant them, carrying around stuff for fixing fences, carrying the potatoes we'd dug up from the paddock to the house to pack them, taking the bagged potatoes to the siding, going into the bush to get wood for our wood stove and many other things.

Dad was still carting cane for other

farmers while we were on the cane farm, but not as much as he previously carted it. I don't know if he only did it for certain farms or if he did a certain amount of truckloads. All I know is he didn't do it as much.

27

After we'd been at the farm for a few years, and I was about eleven or twelve, Dad made me a cubby house. He built it onto the back of the laundry. It had several windows and a door. I made curtains for it out of strips of different coloured material that I cut and hung at the windows. They looked like multicoloured ribbons. Dad bought his kerosene in four-gallon drums. They came in pairs, in a pine box with a lid. Dad used these boxes to make a table and two chairs for my cubby house. He also nailed several of them together for a dresser. None of my furniture was painted. Mum saved the empty grocery containers and I kept them in the dresser to use as pretend food. I also had a white china tea set, with flowers painted on it, that I played with in my cubby house along with a doll I got one Christmas.

I thought my doll was beautiful. She was about eighteen inches tall with a fine straw body covered in pink cotton material and celluloid arms and legs. She had a ceramic head that had ripples in the ceramic for her hair. The ripples were painted brown and she had eyebrows painted on too. She had blue eyes and when she was laid down flat, they closed so she looked like she was sleeping. Her little mouth had red lips that were slightly open, showing her teeth. She had a tiny dummy that fitted in her mouth. When she was turned onto her tummy, she said, 'Ma, Ma'. I called her Una. She came fully dressed, but Mum also made clothes for her. She was big enough she would have fitted into a baby's modern size 000 clothes.

When I first got her I left her in the box. She was too beautiful to take out and risk something happening to her. One day a friend came over and took the doll out of the box. I was so upset. Mum took the doll off my friend and returned her to the box. Eventually I took her out and played with her, but not until a long time had passed.

28

When we had bush fires everyone had to help fight them with a wet sack bag. Except me. I wasn't strong enough so I was given a wet sugar bag to use. Every year we had a bush fire. In the gullies between our house and the river the grass often died off and we sometimes had fires in there. We had to stop the fire from coming up the hill to the house. Sometimes neighbours came over and helped but most of the time we put them out ourselves. There was no garden hose or running water, but we always had a tank of river water at the house where we soaked our bags before going off to fight the fire.

The fires that came in from the direction of the main road, which was about half a mile away, sometimes got close to the house. There was a gully between the house and main road that helped slow them down. I guess the main road was like a highway only we called it a main road in those days. The road had a strip of bitumen down the centre and dirt edges. If a car was coming in the opposite direction both of you had to put one wheel in the dirt to pass each other. If you took the road to the south, after you'd passed through several small towns, you reached Mackay. North took you to Proserpine.

29

When I was twelve Dad made me a doll seat that he screwed onto my bike. It had a pine seat and the sides were a soft metal, which was probably galvanised tin. I think he painted it silver. I was allowed to take my doll Una for rides to my friends' house. All the way there I had to ride with only one hand. Even though Una was strapped into her seat, I held her eyes closed with my other hand so they didn't break. The dirt track was rough and my friends lived about four miles away. If I didn't hold Una's eyes closed they blinked rapidly from being jolted along the track.

My two friends had an older sister who was the eldest child and two older brothers. Their parents were cane farmers too. I didn't get to see them much until I was old enough to ride over by myself because my parents were kept busy looking after the farm. I thought my friends were rich because they had a milk separator, a piano and a nicer house than ours.

30

We had dogs on the cane farm. Dad had two greyhounds. One of them was called Bounce, but I can't recall the name of the other one. I had a blue cattle dog called Biddy. We got her when we moved to the farm. She was supposed to be Dad's dog but she always stayed with me.

One day, when Dad was going down to the paddock, he asked her, "Are you my dog or Joyce's dog?" She walked over and sat at my feet. After that she was mine. If Mum and Dad were down in the paddock, within yelling distance, I tied a note to Biddy's collar and called out to Mum, telling her to call Biddy. After she delivered the note to Mum, Biddy came back to me. I used her to send notes telling Mum things like when I was going to the siding to collect the mail. Biddy was mainly a house dog, but she also brought the cows in. We always had two or three old milkers and then they'd have calves. If it was a heifer we kept it, but we sold the bull calves. Mum was the one who milked them. When I tried I didn't even manage to get enough for a cup of tea.

I often dressed Biddy up with ribbons. One day I was under the mango tree, waiting for it to be time to take smoko to my parents and putting ribbons on Biddy. The cane inspector arrived and Biddy took off, barking at him, her ribbons flying in the wind, streaming all around her. He backed away, afraid she'd bite him.

Another time I was on the way back from delivering smoko when Biddy ran off ahead of me, barking. When I reached home, the cane inspector was standing on a post, Biddy barking at him. I called her to me so he could get down. He was the only person she hated.

31

We didn't get to town very often, but we always went Christmas Eve. It took a couple of hours to drive into town. It was a dirt road until they started putting bitumen down during my teenager years. Christmas Eve we went into town for goodies like soft drinks. We only went into town when we had to. Sometimes it might be once a month, sometimes less. The things we went in for were doctor visits and to get stuff from the chemist. Dances were only once in a blue moon and we didn't go to the movies while we lived on the farm, or even kids' birthday parties, like we did when we'd lived in Gladstone. Everything was too far away and there was always something that needed to be done on the farm. A lot of our time was spent working.

Christmas on the farm was a little boring. We had plenty of food, a lucky Christmas stocking and some toys. But it was just us. No other people came over like they do nowadays. The lucky stocking was shaped like a stocking and filled with trinkets and things like little toys, scribble pads, colouring in books, pencils and in the toe of the stocking there were always lollies. Our Christmas tree was an old oak tree out of the river and we decorated it with crepe paper and anything we could find that looked pretty. We hung pillowcases on the end of our bed for the toys we got Christmas Day. To be able to do this, we had to take them off our pillows first. The pillowcases were made of calico and were two pieces of material sewn together on three sides, with four material tapes at the open end to tie them up so the pillow didn't fall out.

I remember Mum telling me that one Christmas, when she was too old to get toys, she hung her pillowcase up and Santa left her some potatoes and onions. She was very disappointed. When we grew too old for toys there were no presents at all.

At Christmas time, we had to clean out the copper boiler with salt and vinegar. We went down to the river and threw a couple of cups of salt and some vinegar into it. We scrubbed it out using a rag and wiped it over until it shined like a new penny. When it was clean we took it up to the house. It was then filled with clean water and we put the Christmas ham in it. The ham came in a cheesecloth bag that was packed in another bag with wheat husk packing.

We were told Santa came out to our area on the train. Mum always said that if the lights weren't off when his train came through, he wouldn't get off the train and leave presents for us. The train line was the main train line that ran right through to Brisbane and trains went along it at all hours. As well as passenger and freight trains, the cane trains also used the line. Cane trains were normal engines and trucks and travelled along the same track as the rest of the trains. They didn't have the small cane trams with their own track back then.

32

I never saw or had Easter eggs all the time I was on the farm until my sister was married and living in town. I also don't recall any before the farm either, but I was only little. My sister was married in 1938. Near Easter, I went up to collect the mail and my brother-in-law had sent a parcel. It was an Easter egg in a green cardboard box with a red bow. There was one large egg with little chocolates around it all wrapped in green foil. I didn't eat it for a week. I thought I was so lucky.

The goods train stopped at all the little sidings along the way. Monday, Wednesday and Friday mornings it brought the mailbag and also bread to other families. We didn't get bread because Mum made ours. It was the afternoon train coming back through from Calen on a Friday that brought our meat. Calen was halfway between Mackay and where we lived at Noorlah. The river we lived on was the O'Connell River, which passes under the Bruce Highway at one stage. It's north of Mackay and just south of Proserpine. I don't know if there was an actual address for our farm, all our mail was addressed to our private mailbag number. The morning train came around nine-thirty and the afternoon train around four or four-thirty.

33

When I was about thirteen, I went into Proserpine to stay with my sister when her first child was a baby. She was named after me and born when I was twelve. While I was there my sister sent me with a shilling to buy a half loaf of bread every few days. A half loaf was bigger than you get now and was more like a modern day full loaf. It was tall and rose high in the middle. The bread was six pence and with the change from the shilling I was allowed to buy lollies. It was a long walk to the shop. Over a mile. It was a bitumen road with a scattering of houses. The bakery was in the main street of Proserpine along with other shops like a corner store, which wasn't on a corner, and a fruit shop. The fruit shop was where I bought my lollies. I didn't do much in Proserpine. I played with my niece, but I didn't know any other kids in the area. I didn't mind my holidays there, but I got homesick for Mum and sometimes cried myself to sleep at night. I only went for holidays there once in a while.

34

Not far from where we lived was the Andromache River, which eventually flows into the O'Connell River. When they were building the first big O'Connell River Bridge we drove up there on a Sunday and had a picnic with jam sandwiches and patty cakes. We went to see how far along they were in building the bridge. It took a long time for them to build it. One time when we went up there, the workers let us put our initials in some wet cement. The bridge was put where the traffic coming from north and south along the main road would cross. It was only a low bridge and was replaced years later by a higher one that didn't flood so easily.

During the wet season all the farms in the area went under water. You couldn't see a patch of cane. All the houses were built on hills, which I always thought of as the tops of the riverbanks because from our house, the hill went straight down to the cane paddocks and into the river.

35

When we lived on the farm, we got a newspaper called 'The Worker'. It was a free paper and was sent to all the farms. It had agricultural news, amongst other things, and a page called 'The Children's Corner'. We used nicknames and wrote in asking for penfriends, or sent in stories we'd written. I had a lot of penfriends and one of them was about a week younger than me and lived in Bloomsbury. The time eventually came, when I was about fifteen, when he wanted to meet me so he invited me down for the day. I rode my bicycle to the siding and caught the morning train to Bloomsbury.

While I was visiting him I met his older brother Lawrie before taking the afternoon train home. Lawrie, who was eight years older than me, started writing to me and when I was sixteen, Lawrie rode his pushbike out to see me on the farm. It was about twenty-three miles of dirt road with a lot of gullies and hills that made it quite an effort to get there on a bicycle. Lawrie finished work at the railway on a Wednesday afternoon at four o'clock and he went home and had his tea and a bath. Then he rode out to my place and got there about seven o'clock. I was only allowed to sit outside with him until nine o'clock. He also came to visit me on

Sunday afternoon and went home just before dark.

Even though there were dingoes in the bush, Lawrie always came to see me Wednesday night. It was dark on the road home as there weren't any streetlights. Lawrie had a square bike light that fit on his handlebars and was run by a battery. It was about as bright as the modern two battery torch with a standard bulb you can buy from the supermarket. There was no way for me to know if he got home safe as we had no phone for him to ring us.

Lawrie's father was a fettler on the line and every morning he checked the railway lines and delivered Lawrie's love letters. There was a spot at our siding where he hid the letters Lawrie wrote and where I left my reply. A fettler was someone who repaired and maintained the railway lines.

36

Lawrie and I were engaged for about four years and once, during our engagement we went to the circus. It was about twenty-six miles from our farm to Proserpine where the circus was held. The man who eventually married Lawrie's sister collected Lawrie and me from the main road. We walked the quarter of a mile from the farm to meet him there. He had an open truck and his parents, Lawrie's father, brother, sister and a few other kids went with us. We arrived in Proserpine on dark. During interval time Lawrie came back into the tent, after he'd been outside a few minutes, laughing. His father, who'd gone out to the toilet, had fallen over a camel that had been sitting down at the side of the tent. During the interval, they sold food like hot dogs, fairy floss and toffee apples. I didn't get home to the farm until the early hours of the morning. It was such a long drive to go to the circus. Cars and trucks didn't go as fast as they do now and the roads were nowhere near as good.

37

I married Lawrie when I was twenty-one, in 1947, and we went to live in Bloomsbury for about two and a half years. That was also the year Lawrie's dad died. I had my first child in 1949. I stayed with Lawrie's mum, in Proserpine, a couple of weeks before he was due and she called the ambulance to take me to the hospital when it was time to have him. In those days the mother went to the delivery room on her own. After his birth, I returned with him to Bloomsbury on the goods train.

Lawrie worked in the railway at Bloomsbury. He repaired the line and bridges from Bloomsbury in each direction for so many miles. Every morning two people went off on the pumper to check the lines. The pumper was an open tray wagon that went along the train lines and was driven by two men pumping a lever. The men had to make sure no trees had fallen across the line and nothing else was wrong.

38

After we'd lived in Bloomsbury awhile, we returned to the farm, where Mum and my brothers lived and worked the cane farm. Dad had since moved to Rockhampton and returned to carpentry. Lawrie developed a double hernia from lifting bundles of cane and throwing them onto the truck. We were only at the farm for a few months and by 1952 we lived in Proserpine where my second child was born. Proserpine was also where my other two children were born.

While we were on the farm my oldest celebrated his first birthday. During the years I'd lived there as a child, the only birthday cakes I had were for my sixteenth and twenty-first birthdays. I started a new tradition that year on the farm. For all my children's birthdays, while they lived at home, I made sure they had a birthday cake to celebrate reaching another year. My own children and grandchildren have carried on that tradition.

Australian Currency Pre 1966

12 pence to a shilling

20 shillings to a pound

Coins

Halfpenny 1911-1966

Penny 1911-1966

Silver Threepence 1910-1966

Sixpence 1910-1966

Shilling 1910-1966

Florin 1910-1966

Notes

10 Shillings 1913-1966

One Pound 1913-1966

Five Pounds 1913-1966

Ten Pounds 1914-1966

Twenty Pounds 1913-1966

Fifty Pounds 1914-1966

One Hundred Pounds 1914-1966

One Thousand Pounds 1914–1966
(inter-bank uses)

Measurements

Imperial Measurements

Length

12 inches = 1 foot

3 feet = 1 yard

1760 yards = 1 mile

Volume

20 fluid ounces = 1 pint

2 pints = 1 quart

4 quarts = 1 gallon

Mass

16 ounces = 1 pound

14 pounds = 1 stone

Imperial to Metric

Length

1 inch = 2.54 centimetres

1 foot = 30.48 centimetres

1 yard = 91.44 centimetres

1 mile = 1.609 kilometres

Volume

1 fluid ounce = 28.413 millilitres

1 pint = 0.568 litres

1 quart = 1.136 litres

1 gallon = 4.546 litres

Mass

1 ounce = 28.349 grams

1 pound = 0.453 kilograms

1 stone = 6.350 kilograms

Australian Events

The following are some of the events happening in Australia leading up to and during Joyce's first forty years.

1901   Australia becomes a federation, Edmund Barton becomes the first Prime Minister and the Australian National Flag is flown for the first time.

1903   The High Court of Australia is established.

1908   Canberra is chosen as the capital of Australia.

1909   First powered aeroplane flight in Australia.

1911   The Royal Australian Navy is founded.

1914   Australian soldiers are sent to World War I.

1918   World War I ends 11th November. 60,000 Australians dead.

1920   Qantas Airlines founded at Winton, Queensland and Bonds start manufacturing their men's athletic singlets.

1921   Edith Cowan is the first Australian woman elected to parliament.

1923   Vegemite first produced.

1924   Compulsory voting brought in for Federal elections.

1926   First Miss Australian contest held. **Joyce born**.

1927   Bert Hinkler makes the first successful flight from Britain to Australia. Charles Kingsford Smith makes the first successful flight from United States to Australia.

1929   The Great Depression lasts until 1932.

1930   Donald Bradman scores world record in cricket and Phar Lap wins his only Melbourne Cup race.

1931   Sir Douglas Mawson charts 4,000 miles of Antarctic's coastline and claims forty-two percent for Australia. **Joyce five-years-old.**

1932   Construction of Sydney Harbour Bridge is completed.

1935   The cane toad is imported into Queensland and becomes a pest.

1936   The last thylacine dies. **Joyce ten-years-old.**

1937   The radio series 'Dad and Dave' begins.

1939   Victoria is hit by the Black Friday bushfires that claim seventy-one lives and Australia enters World War II.

1940   Howard Florey and a team of scientists develop penicillin.

1941   **Joyce fifteen-years-old.**

1942 National Daylight Savings introduced as a war measure.

1943 Damien Parer's 'Kokoda Front Line' was the first Australian film to win an Oscar.

1944 Pharmaceutical Benefits Scheme introduced to provide subsidised medicine to all Australians.

1945 World War II ends and Australia becomes a founding member of the United Nations. The Sydney to Hobart Yacht Race is held for the first time.

1946 Introduction of the post-war immigration scheme. **Joyce twenty-years-old.**

1948 Holden starts manufacturing first Australian designed and built car and Donald Bradman retires from cricket. Australia becomes a signatory to the Universal Declaration of Human Rights.

1950   Australian troops sent to the Korean War until 1953.

1951   Australia signs the ANZUS treaty with the United States and New Zealand. **Joyce twenty-five-years-old.**

1954   Newly crowned Queen Elizabeth II, along with Prince Philip, makes a royal visit to Australia.

1956   Black and white television launched in Australia and the sixteenth Summer Olympics are held in Melbourne. Edna Everage is introduced to the Australian stage. **Joyce thirty-years-old.**

1959   Construction begins on the Sydney Opera House.

1960   The Reserve Bank Of Australia is established.

1961   **Joyce thirty-five-years-old.**

1966   Australian currency is changed to dollars and cents. **Joyce forty-years-old.**

Acknowledgements

Thank you to all those involved in the creation of this book, in particular Grandma. It meant a lot to me as a child that you always had time to tell me your stories.

To The Reader

If you enjoyed this book, why not consider leaving a review to help other readers discover it too? Reader engagement is one of the few ways that lets an author know readers want more books in a particular series or genre. So leave a review and tell friends, not only about this book but also about other ones you've enjoyed, so you can continue to enjoy books by your favourite authors for years to come.

Dreams are meant to be lived,

Avril.

About The Author

Avril is an Australian author who lives with her family on acreage in South East Queensland. She writes mostly young adult speculative fiction, but has been known to dabble in other genres. You can find more information about her at her website www.avrilsabine.com where you can also subscribe to her newsletter to be kept informed about new releases, current projects, blog posts and exclusive news.

Titles By Avril Sabine

Stories about strong characters and characters who discover their strengths.

SERIES

Assassins Of The Dead- Young Adult Fantasy/Paranormal

Book 1: Dark Blade

Book 2: Dragon Touched

Book 3: Society Against Vampires

Book 4: King's Request

Dragon Blood- Young Adult Urban Fantasy (with elements of romance)

(5 book series)

Book 1: Pliethin

Book 2: Wyvern

Book 3: Surety

Book 4: Knight

Book 5: Mage

Dragon Mage- Young Adult Urban Fantasy (with elements of romance)

(Series two of Dragon Blood series)

Book 1: Promise

Dragon Blood Chronicles- Young Adult Urban Fantasy (with elements of romance)

(Companion stand alone series to Dragon Blood)

Book 1: Oath

Book 2: Betrayed

Guardians Of The Round Table- Young Adult Fantasy LitRPG

(Co-written with Storm and Rhys Petersen)

Book 1: Dexterity Fail

Book 2: Goblin Boots

Book 3: Singed Feathers

Book 4: Frog Mage

Book 5: Crystal Mine

Book 6: Cursed Harp

Rosie's Rangers- Young Adult Western Steampunk

(6 book series)

Book 1: Justice

Book 2: Vengeance

Book 3: Treachery

Book 4: Accused

Book 5: Wanted

Book 6: Corruption

Mark Of Kings- Children's Fantasy

(Upper middle grade/preteen)

(4 book series)

Book 1: The Arena

Book 2: The Island

Book 3: The Assassin

Book 4: The King

STAND ALONE SERIES

Demon Hunters- Young Adult

Urban Fantasy/Horror (with elements of romance)

Book 1: Blood Sacrifice

Book 2: Retribution

Book 3: Tainted

Book 4: Premonition

Book 5: Cursed

Book 6: Feud

Book 7: Extrication

Plea Of The Damned- Young Adult Urban Fantasy/Paranormal

(6 book series)

Book 1: Forgive Me Lucy

Book 2: Forgive Me Aiden

Book 3: Forgive Me Jena

Book 4: Forgive Me Kobe

Book 5: Forgive Me Marti

Book 6: Forgive Me Dawson

Realms Of The Fae- Young Adult Urban Fantasy (with elements of romance)

The Sword (short story in Like A Girl Anthology)

Heart Of Stone

Book 1: A Debt Owed

Book 2: Marked By The Hunt

Book 3: The Magic Collector

Book 4: An Unexpected Betrayal

Book 5: Imprisoned By Iro

Fairytales Retold (Short Stories)

Snow-White And Rose-Red

The Twelve Brothers

The Light Princess

Beauty And The Beast

Sleeping Beauty

Aschenputtel

The Golden Bird

The Frog Prince

The Death Of Koshchei The Deathless

Myths And Legends Retold (Short Stories)

Ion, Son Of Apollo

Sir Gawain And The Maid With The Narrow Sleeves

Princess Ilse, The Giant's Daughter

YOUNG ADULT NOVELS

Young Adult Fantasy (with elements of romance)

Elf Sight

Earth Bound

Young Adult Urban Fantasy

Stone Warrior (with elements of romance)

The Jungle Inside

Young Adult Contemporary (with elements of romance)

Through Your Eyes

The Ugly Stepsister

Perfect Little Princess

Young Adult Contemporary/ Paranormal

Whispers In The Dark (with

elements of romance and same sex relationships)

Over Too Soon (with elements of romance)

Young Adult Sci-Fi

Experiment X-One-Six (Urban Sci-Fi/Superheroes)

An Endless Dawn (Post Apocalyptic Sci-Fi)

CHILDREN'S BOOKS

Dragon Lord (Preteen/early teens) (Fantasy)

The Irish Wizard (Upper middle grade) (Urban Fantasy)

SHORT STORIES

Urban Fantasy

Eternally Late

Dealings With Joe

Glimpses (short story in That Moment When Anthology)

Contemporary

The Brat Next Door

Fantasy LitRPG

(Set in the same world as Guardians Of The Round Table Series)

Tales Of Inadon 1: The Disc (Co-written with Storm and Rhys Petersen) (short story in Game On! Anthology)

Post Apocalyptic Sci-Fi

Compulsive Directive

NONFICTION

A Year Of Weekly Writing Exercises (Creative Writing)

Cooking For Families With Allergies (Cooking) (Co-written with Storm Petersen)

Tell Me A Story, Grandma (Memoir)

For the most up to date details on available titles visit:

www.avrilsabine.com/books/bibliography

Disclaimer

This is a work of creative nonfiction. The events portrayed are done so long after the fact and as such rely on memory. They have been recreated to the best of the ability of those involved.

www.ingramcontent.com/pod-product-compliance
Lightning Source LLC
Chambersburg PA
CBHW021439080526
44588CB00009B/594